Messy Church® is a fas
continues to engage and
thousands of people ou
context. Week by week we are seeing new Messy Churches starting across the UK, as well as in other countries around the world.

Messy Church is resourced, supported and enabled by BRF as one of its core ministries. It is largely funded by grants and donations. We need your help to continue to enable the growth and ongoing development of Messy Churches, large and small, wherever they are found.

Could you or your church help BRF's Messy Church ministry continue to make a difference through giving and prayer? www.messychurch.org.uk/support-messy-church

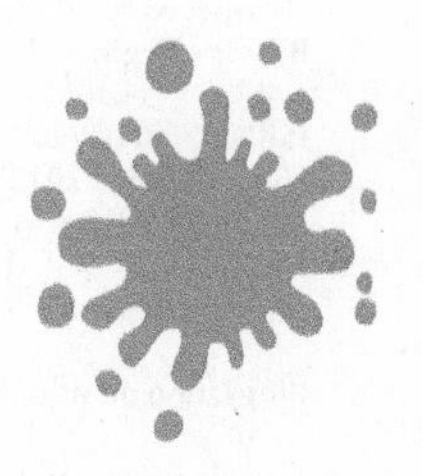

Published by
The Bible Reading Fellowship
15 The Chambers, Vineyard
Abingdon OX14 3FE
United Kingdom
Tel: +44 (0)1865 319700
Email: enquiries@brf.org.uk
Website: www.brf.org.uk
BRF is a Registered Charity

ISBN 978 0 85746 055 4
First published 2012
Reprinted 2012 (twice), 2014
10 9 8 7 6 5 4 3

A catalogue record for this book is available from the British Library

Printed and bound by CPI Group (UK) Ltd, Croydon, CR0 4YY

How to run your very own Messy Nativity Advent project

Jane Leadbetter

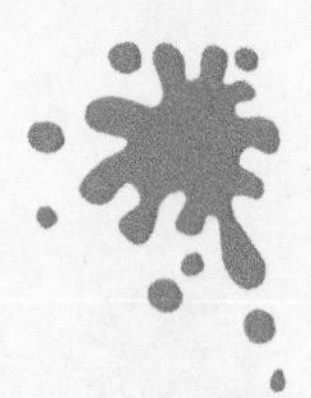

To my husband, Ian.

How wonderful to receive your constant love, support and companionship over the years!

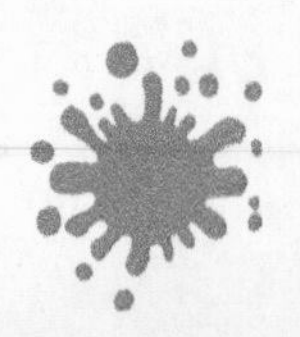

Contents

Foreword

Very early on the last Saturday morning before Christmas, after the first unexpectedly heavy snowfall of winter, I tentatively found my way to the local BBC radio station.

I was to explain the Messy Nativity that we were planning for later in the day to their audience. Half the radio production team had failed to make it through the snow to work. We feared the worst. However, although we were much fewer in number than we'd planned, our indomitable Messy Nativity production team represented several different Christian agencies: our Diocesan Children's Work Adviser; Mission in the Economy Chaplaincy Providers; Youth with a Mission; the city centre Pioneer Minister; Liverpool Anglican Cathedral's Sunday school choir and last but not least, the Mothers' Union! It was a truly multi-agency happening.

More importantly, in the city centre market and shopping precinct where we staged our production we engaged such diverse cast members—an angel from the cold meats counter, a Joseph from the mobile phone shop, a props assistant from the antiques stall... Magnificent chaos and great fun! How could such diverse people who have very little or no connection with 'church' come together and manage to share the spirit of Christmas?

Messy Nativity allowed them, and those who looked on, to be reminded of the real meaning of Christmas in a most memorable way—with photos to prove it. They learnt that Jesus Christ is the gift to end all gifts, non-returnable and with no sell-by date, given amid the mess and chaos of a stable in an oppressed society. Only God could make that magnificent!

Messy Nativity left a new trail of fresh footprints for those who have never thought of going his way before. May it continue to point the way for others to follow.

Revd Jean Flood, Mission in the Economy

Introduction

I am not a shopaholic. Indeed, normally, you have to drag me to the shops, kicking and screaming. I don't understand all of that BOGOF or coupon jargon. In my mind you either want it or you don't. So, as Christmas 2009 approached and the present list stared me in the face, I just had to grin and bear it, and off to Liverpool ONE shopping centre I went—160 shops, more than 20 bars and restaurants, a huge cinema and a park packed with Christmas attractions.

As I shuffled around the shops, I looked for evidence of the Real Christmas. I spotted Christmas decorations: robins, snowmen, snowflakes, penguins, puddings, stockings, holly and mistletoe. Everywhere there were garlands, miles and miles of green boughs adorned with baubles and lights. I also spotted Santas (or Father Christmases if you prefer)—large hanging ones, giant blown-up versions, smaller 'nodding head' or talking Santas—but I couldn't find Jesus anywhere.

National TV and radio coverage of the build-up to Christmas during Advent advertised many seasonal events, and I heard more and more about 'WinterFests' or festive grottoes. Traditional school Nativity plays were being revamped to incorporate penguins and lobsters! It was political correctness gone mad. Was the city of Liverpool sliding down this slippery route of squeezing out the Real meaning of Christmas? I sensed it was. But could I do anything about it? How could I help to introduce or reintroduce Jesus into people's lives as they shopped for their bargains and presents for their loved ones?

I once went to see a production of Lloyd Webber/ Rice's *Jesus Christ Superstar*. During the performance I overheard a family behind me saying that they couldn't understand why someone was hammering nails into the hands of Jesus. Since then I have never undersold the stories of the Nativity and Easter. I feel that we can never assume that all generations are familiar with the real reason for celebrating Christmas and Easter, and why we buy presents and chocolate eggs.

In this book I share a story of hope. Jesus said to his disciples, 'Go throughout the whole world and preach the gospel to the whole human race.' So why, even at Christmas, is this becoming so hard to do, when the story of Jesus' birth is gradually being squeezed out of our towns and cities, amongst the hustle and bustle of Christmas shopping, during the season of Advent? When the Real meaning of Christmas is being replaced with Santa's Magical Kingdom and WinterFests? How can we bring Jesus back into our communities during Advent?

I pray that this book will inspire you to take action and enjoy the challenge of linking Messy Sheep with the Nativity story and getting Jesus baaaack in town!

Jane Leadbetter

Chapter 1: The Messy Nativity Project

I coordinate a Messy Church in South Liverpool. We particularly aim to invite families who choose not to come to a Sunday service in church, so once a month we hold Messy Church on a Saturday afternoon. Messy Church is a time for all ages to come together to be creative with crafts and activities, to celebrate and to eat together. It is centred on Christ, and from the moment you enter a messy space you are worshipping.

Messy Church is engaging and fun and growing rapidly all over the world. There are Messy Churches on weekdays and at weekends, incorporating lunch times, tea times, breakfasts. They are held in school buildings, church halls, churches and community halls. At my Messy Church we are always looking for different ways to fill the monthly gap. We have had a presence at a local market and Fun Days, and given out take-home sheets to families.

You may wonder how this links with the Messy Nativity. I am also the Messy Church Regional Coordinator for the Merseyside area. I discovered that the Diocese of Liverpool Mothers' Union was planning events to celebrate its 120th anniversary in 2010. Could I help them with any projects? A summer day on the beach was planned, but what about something to end the year? Could it be an Advent project? After discussions we decided to link the Mothers' Union and Messy Church, as both organisations work with families, and to find a workable project that would promote the Nativity story. A new Christian pioneer ministry was taking off in Liverpool city centre—River in the City—and I felt God wanting me to include this. I also discovered a group of city-centre chaplains, doing quiet and wonderful work in various ways and with links to Liverpool Mission in the Economy. I wondered how they felt Christmas in the city centre was developing.

Then my daughter informed me of how knitting, for all ages, was on trend.

I don't knit. Well, I could if pushed, but it had been years since I tried to knit the proverbial scarf and became bored with it before finishing. So I had no idea how popular knitting had become once again. Knitting groups and clubs were popping up everywhere. University students started 'knit and natters'. Libraries, pubs and cafes became regular venues, and knitting blogs and websites were on the increase.

So the Messy Nativity project grew out of Christmas shopping, Mothers' Union celebrations, Messy Church and creative knitting! At the heart of the project was the desire to spread the story of Jesus' birth. As the project aimed to run during the season of Advent, I was conscious of how busy everyone already was and that I wouldn't be able to create a large team to deliver a large project. As I worked full-time, the project had to be easy to set up and easy to manage. So I split the project into three parts:

1. **The Messy Nativity Sheep Trail** (spot the knitted sheep in shops);
2. **The Messy Nativity Set Journey** (the Posada idea with added knitted sheep);
3. **The Messy Street Nativity** (tell the Nativity story in the street using drama/script).

Featuring in all three parts of the project were sheep!

I enjoy working with people and teams, and the Messy Nativity project allowed me to approach people and include them in the project: the Diocese of Liverpool Mothers' Union, Liverpool ONE management and their chaplain, River in the City, Mission in the Economy. This may sound like lots of organisations, but I really only worked with one key person from each, and on different parts of the project.

God led me to people who also had a heart for spreading the story of Jesus' birth and together we piloted the project in Liverpool. But this project can happen anywhere: in a city, or local shops, a retail park, a market, a village, anywhere. You can do the whole project or just use one part of it. You can work with others or on your own. First of all, pray about it. I hope that the following chapters will give you the practical help and know-how, but first you must decide why you want to do it. Do you need to put Jesus back in your town during Advent? Prepare yourself for an opportunity to create a messy community in Jesus' name.

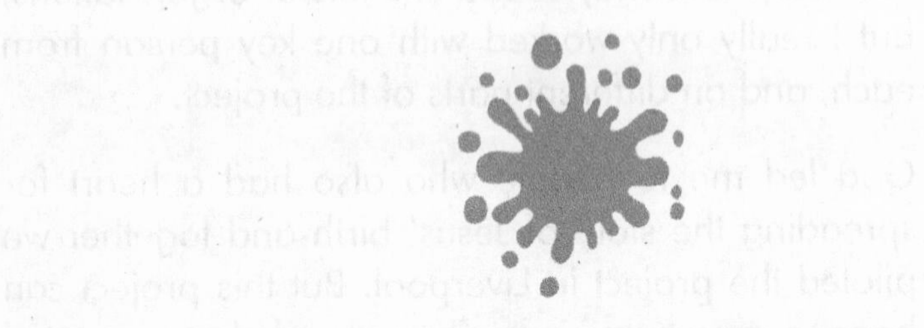

Chapter 2: The Messy Nativity Sheep Trail

Liverpool is famous for the Beatles, two cathedrals, two football teams and lots, lots more, including (in case you are interested) the first council houses built in Europe!

The city is also well known for its trails, and I don't just mean heritage trails. The Superlambanana Trail was created for Liverpool's year as European Capital of Culture in 2008. One hundred and twenty-five Superlambanana sculptures were placed around the Merseyside region and families and individuals became dedicated 'spotters', armed with leaflets helping them to try to find them all. Tourists visited Liverpool to spend whole weekends hunting for the bright, individually decorated sculptures, and the project was deemed a huge success.

The following year another trail was created by an art company—Go Penguins! This time 142 five-foot penguins, individually decorated, invited you to hunt for them on a Winter's Trail. This was so popular that other cities and towns around the country engaged in similar trails. There were rhinos in Chester, superdragons in Newport, elephants in Norwich, hippos in Rutland and lions in Northampton.

So, could this trail idea be scaled down to something that would invite families to explore city-centre shops while they were Christmas shopping, and at the same time somehow engage them in the Real meaning of Christmas?

Using animals on these trails, including fantasy animals, seemed to have captured the imaginations of all ages around these cities. Which animal could link up Christmas shopping with the Nativity story? More importantly, how could any animals be produced without costing lots of money? What size should they be? What should they be made from? Who was going to make them?

My determination to make this project a cheap and exciting one probably stemmed from my experience as a Beaver Scout leader, and also from creating trails in Liverpool Anglican Cathedral. Sometimes it is the simplest methods that work best. My daughter Sarah, a knitter, helped me, a non-knitter, to understand how more people would want to engage in simple knitting rather than complicated patterns. So to choose the donkey or ox from the Nativity story would be more problematic than, say, to choose a sheep. Sarah convinced me that a sheep was the easiest Nativity animal to knit and that beginners could be involved as well as experts!

Messy thought

Sheep are messy and dirty. Their woolly fleeces are messy, dirty, and clumpy. To be spun into yarn the wool must first be sorted and then cleaned with hot water and detergent, a process called scouring. How appropriate that we chose a messy animal for our project! Sheep are vulnerable and are easily led astray. They need constant care and commitment. Is this a challenge for each one of us—to shepherd God's flock particularly at a time when our belief is being tested, being squeezed out of one of the most significant times in the Christian calendar—Christmas?

So far it looked as if we could keep costs down by knitting the sheep, and we could involve knitters from all walks of life. But how many should we knit, and what size? The thought of knitting 142 five-foot sheep terrified me! After visiting a Liverpool ONE shop I realised that the sheep needed to be able to balance on a shelf or stand in a display area, and that every inch of space was expertly used by the managers to create a selling opportunity. I hoped and prayed that the shops would allow us to take a small space for a sheep.

Sarah created a pattern for a knitted sheep measuring 20 cm in height. A prototype was made (see page 26).

I was amazed by the number of people who offered to knit sheep, and became a delighted messy shepherdess. Work colleagues and their families knitted; Mothers' Union branches and churches knitted; Knit and Natter groups knitted. Sheep arrived at my sheepfold in parcels through the post, in bags left in my home porch and via the Mothers' Union office. We had so many that we could share them with lots of churches taking part in the project.

Some sheep were personalised, knitted in bright colours and named. Some sheep on my work desk magically changed position overnight! As I arrived at work each morning, I was greeted by the sight of sheep jumping over fences, or baa-coded, or grazing on real grass, or in a Little Bo Peep nursery rhyme pose. I seemed to have created a community of sheep taking over Liverpool!

I had absolutely no idea how sheep would capture people's imaginations. Sheep are... well, sheep are just woolly and sort of round in shape, I thought. Yet, once knitted, they become cute, in need of a name, and they need messy friends. On the Messy Sheep Trail in Liverpool city shops I found store managers holding in-house competitions to name their sheep; one knitted sheep was named after a manager's father; another was named after a Christmas decoration. Some sheep 'travelled' around the store each day, and one store insisted on 'dressing' their sheep themselves.

When I returned to the stores, after the trail, to collect the knitted sheep, I found staff reluctant to give back their knitted friends, pleading with me to let them keep them and to create an Easter Trail so that the store could keep their knitted friend all year round. Some staff were close to tears as I exited down the escalator with their sheep, and one store deliberately made their sheep so hard to reach that they quoted health and safety reasons for them to keep it! Another shop wanted the knitted sheep to have their own website…

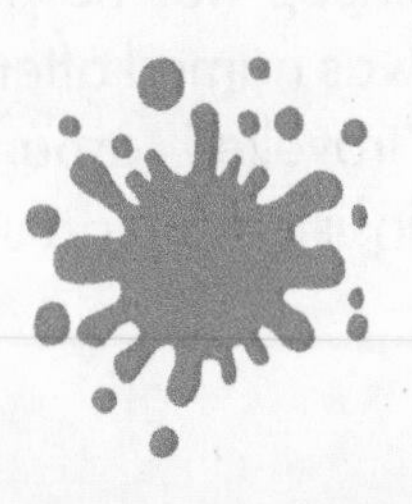

Trail action plan

It's time to arrange some meetings with people to get the project going! There's no avoiding it. You have to gain permission for most ideas, but where should you start?

Early planning checklist:

- Pray.
- Plan well in advance of Advent.
- Choose family-friendly shops to approach.
- If the shops are part of a shopping complex, contact the complex managing staff for a meeting to share your idea.
- Emphasise that you will be doing all of the work and that you just need permission to work together.
- Emphasise that the shops will hopefully benefit financially, as the trail will encourage people of all ages to enter their shop and increase their footfall during the Advent period.
- Explain that the Nativity story will be printed on a trail leaflet. Don't try to hide the fact that this is a Christian project.

Messy preparation:

- When you have permission, visit each chosen shop and arrange to see the manager. It is very important to take a knitted sheep with you so that they can see what you are proposing.
- Invite each shop to choose a name for their sheep. This could happen on the spot or take a few days.
- Obtain contact details for each chosen shop. Leave your own contact details.
- Give each shop a start and finishing date for the trail.
- If any shop offers a prize for a trail competition, identify a place where a prize draw box could be placed.
- Get knitting! Pray for donations of wool and knitting needles. Create a small knitting team and try to stick to the same pattern!
- Produce enough sheep for the chosen shops plus a spare in case of a sheep 'wandering'.
- Decide how you will decorate and place names on the knitted sheep (tinsel, bells, luggage labels, ribbon, etc.).
- Remind shops that each sheep needs a name. Write the name clearly on a label and attach it to the sheep.
- Create a small standalone notice or label to place alongside each knitted sheep in the shops. This

should advertise the Messy Nativity Sheep Trail and have your contact details on the reverse in case of emergency.

- Create a trail leaflet (see page 29). List each shop/department and leave space for the sheep name to be completed. Allow space for the Nativity story text and, if wished, a Nativity maze/wordsearch and colouring picture. Include any organisation logos and websites, together with acknowledgments and thanks. This is a good opportunity to advertise your church or Messy Church and any upcoming events.
- **Visit www.brfonline.org.uk/messy-church/ for free template downloads of the leaflet and other resource sheets in this book**.
- If you wish to add a prize draw competition to the trail, include space for the participant's details and take advice on database/privacy policy declaration text. Design the leaflet so that the participant can tear down the dotted line and place one side of the leaflet in the prize draw box. The second side, with the Nativity story on, can be taken home.
- Choose a prize draw date.
- Pray for donations towards leaflet photocopying.
- Arrange a trail launch.
- Create a trail poster for the window of each participating shop.

- Create a prize draw box if needed.
- Advertise!

Process after the trail launch:

- Regularly check that each shop has enough leaflets.
- Advertise the prize draw if necessary.
- Collect any prizes/vouchers from shops if offered.
- Hold the prize draw.
- Contact each winner and arrange prize collection.
- When a winner is contacted, ask for feedback on the trail, and copy any positive remarks to use for any future advertising.
- After the trail end date, collect all knitted sheep.
- Send a thankyou card to each participating shop and ask for feedback on the trail.
- Thank God.

What could go messy?

- If you plan this project months in advance, remind the management of the shops or shopping complex nearer the launch date in case of a change of staff.
- If a shop forgets to find a name for their sheep, have one ready for the launch date.

- On the launch date, make a trial run of the trail to make sure everything is in place in each shop.
- Don't make the trail unnecessarily long by placing shops next to each other on the leaflet which are actually miles apart.
- Don't be tempted to add too many participating shops to the trail. If the trail takes too long it will add a negative feel to a happy shopping day.

Messy memory

There's always one troublesome sheep! Her name was Sheila. She was named by and placed in Waterstones bookstore in the children's department. The only phone call I received about the trail was when a family rang to complain that they couldn't find the knitted sheep in Waterstones. When I arrived at the store Sheila had been found at last. She had hidden herself behind a book display on a high shelf. I suppose it was inevitable that one of the sheep would get lost!

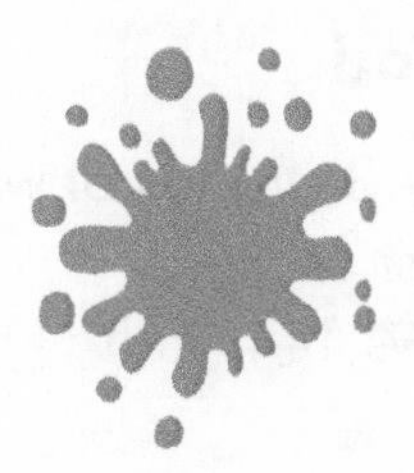

Large sheep knitting pattern (Sarah Leadbetter)

You will need:

100g white/cream Aran wool (make into three small balls)
50g black/brown Aran wool
9mm or 10mm needles
Toy stuffing
Googly eyes, buttons or felt circles

Body (all in garter stitch)

Use 3 strands of white/cream wool together
Cast on 15
Rows 1 and 2: Knit
Row 3: Increase in every stitch (30 sts)
Row 4: Knit
Row 5: *K5, increase 1* 6 times (36 sts)
Rows 6–30: Knit
Row 31: (K2tog) to end
Cast off

Head

Use 3 strands of white/cream wool together
Cast on 20
Rows 1–4: Knit

Row 5: Increase into every stitch (40sts)
Row 6–9: Knit
Change to black/grey wool
Row 10: Purl
Row 11: *K2, K2tog* to end
Row 12: Purl
Row 13: *K1, K2tog* to end
Row 14: Purl
Row 15: *K2tog* to end
Thread yarn through remaining stitches

Legs

Use 3 strands of black/grey wool together
Cast on 10
Rows 1, 3 and 5: Knit
Rows 2, 4 and 6: Purl
Row 7: *K2tog* to end
Thread yarn through remaining stitches

Ears

Use 3 strands of black/grey wool together
Cast on 4
Cast off

Assembly

Sew the body of the sheep. Keep the neck end open. Sew up the side of the head, leaving the neck open.

Stuff both body and head and sew the head straight on to the body.
Do the same with the legs, then sew on the ears and stitch on a cute face!
Use stick-on googly eyes, buttons or felt circles for the eyes.
Make a small pompom for the tail (optional). Create whatever kind of tail you like.

Small sheep knitting pattern suggestions

I'm sure you have your favourite patterns, or your granny or neighbour has one to share. But if not, try:

www.flutterbypatch.blogspot.com

www.barnabasinschools.org.uk/pdfs/biblestorybags1.pdf

or contact your local Mothers' Union office for their Knitted Nativity Pattern.

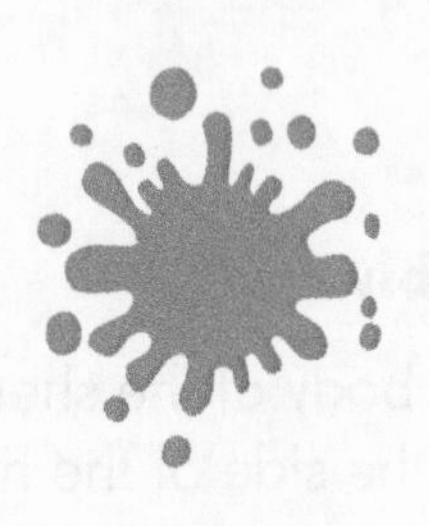

Messy Nativity Sheep Trail

One of the Liverpool ONE shepherds wants to go and see baby Jesus, but he can't find all his sheep! He knows that he went into these shops—will you help him find his missing sheep?

Name of shop ________________ Name of shop ________________

Name of shop ________________ Name of shop ________________

Name of shop ________________ Name of shop ________________

Name of shop ________________ Name of shop ________________

Name of shop ________________ Name of shop ________________

Name of shop ________________ Name of shop ________________

When you find a sheep you can write its name in the spaces above.

The Christmas Story

On 25 December we celebrate Christmas, the birthday of Jesus who was called Christ...

Before Jesus was born, his parents, Mary and Joseph, went to a town called Bethlehem. It was very busy and they couldn't find anywhere to stay. A friendly innkeeper let them sleep in his stable with the animals. Jesus was born, and Mary wrapped him in cloths and put him in the manger. A star appeared in the sky over the stable.

Out in the fields, some shepherds were looking after their sheep when suddenly an angel appeared. The shepherds were very scared. The angel told the shepherds not to be scared because he had brought good news. He told them that Jesus had been born and that he would be the person who would save the world. He told the shepherds to go and see Jesus. Then there were lots more angels who sang glory to God and peace on earth.

The shepherds went to see the baby Jesus. They knelt down in front of the manger and were very happy that they had found the one who had been sent by God. When they left, they told everybody they could find about Jesus and about how he was going to save the world.

Later on, some wise men came from the East to see Jesus. They brought special gifts because they knew that Jesus was a king. They were surprised that he had been born in a stable and not in a palace. They worshipped Jesus and gave him gifts of gold, frankincense and myrrh.

And so...

Each Christmas we celebrate Jesus being born. God gave us Jesus as a present to show that he loves us. Each Christmas we give each other presents to show people that we love them.

Thank you for taking part in the Messy Nativity Sheep Trail.

Have you found the names of all the sheep?

Have you written their names in the spaces?

Would you like to enter a prize draw?

The Messy Nativity Sheep Trail is an activity made in collaboration with ....
....
....

So what do you do now?

1. Tear along the dotted line
2. Take home the colouring picture side of the leaflet
3. Clearly enter your details below
4. Place this side of your leaflet in the prize draw box at:

.... [Name of shop/building/floor/address]

Name (print clearly): ....

Contact telephone number: ....

Email: ....

Date of birth: ....

A prize draw will take place on .... [Date/time]

Chapter 3:
The Messy Nativity Set Journey

Some of you may have already heard of or experienced a Posada. This is a Mexican tradition where, leading up to Christmas, people dressed as characters from the Nativity story visit homes re-enacting the Nativity and sharing the story. A modern version has been devised by the Church Army, who since 2000 have offered resources to help parishes to send a Nativity Set around homes in their community. As each home hosts the set they share the prayer and story with one another before passing the set on to the next host.

What a wonderful opportunity to help families and individuals practically engage with the Nativity story! The Nativity Set in itself is a magnificent resource, but to know that it is on a journey and that each household plays a significant part in its journey adds to the anticipation during the season of Advent as we look forward to the excitement and celebration of Jesus' birthday.

We decided to use the Posada idea as part of our Messy Nativity project. The Liverpool Mothers' Union advertised the Advent project through their branches, and we made the downloadable rota sheet and resources available on their website (see pages 42 to 45).

This part of the Messy Nativity Project can be delivered through churches, Messy Churches, schools and neighbourhoods. In addition to the Nativity Set

I suggest each church gives a small knitted sheep to each host household. (See page 28 for pattern suggestions.) This sheep can be retained as the Nativity Set is passed on, and can be a reminder of the Nativity story and/or an invitation to join in with a Christmas gathering or event, for example on Christmas Eve, when everyone who has received the Nativity Set in their home attends a service in church to celebrate the end of its journey.

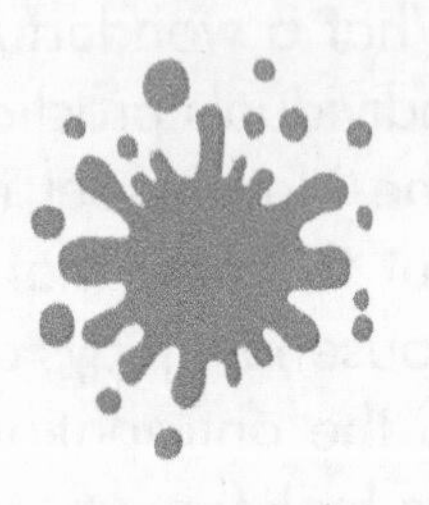

Organising a Messy Nativity Set Journey

Here's an overview of the main stages:

Preparation:

Through November promote the Messy Nativity Project, complete the journey rota, find a suitable Nativity Set, photocopy Nativity Story sheets, knit lots of small sheep!

Advent Sunday:

The Nativity Set, together with a bag of small knitted sheep, is handed to the first host family on the journey rota.

Advent Season:

The Nativity Set is passed from home to home, each home retaining a Nativity Story sheet plus one small knitted sheep.

Christmas Eve:

The Nativity Set is brought to church to a suitable all-age service or event.

Preparation:

- Well in advance of the project invite knitters to knit small sheep. You will need approximately 30 in total, which includes a few spare in case of lost sheep!
- Publicise Messy Nativity and emphasise that the Nativity Set can visit all types of household, large or small families or elderly people living alone.
- Encourage people to host the Nativity Set by adding their names, addresses and telephone numbers to the journey rota.
- If there is a surplus of host households, suggest that people double up, with one household inviting another to come round when the Nativity Set arrives.
- If there are insufficient hosts, the Nativity Set can spend more than one night in a house or could visit a local school, hospital or care home.
- Choose or purchase a suitably robust Nativity Set for the journey (see page 41 for suggestions).
- Decide upon arrangements within your parish/ church for collecting and delivering the Nativity Set.
- Plan a suitable all-age service or event on Christmas Eve to invite the Nativity Set to be returned to church. Ideas could include a Christingle Service, a Carol Service, a Crib Service, a Nativity Service, a Jesus Party, a Sheep Stall with sheep crafts, or a Shepherds' Party.

Advent Sunday:

The first host receives the Nativity Set, a small knitted sheep and the Nativity Story sheet. You may wish to incorporate this launch of the journey in a Sunday church service.

Advent Season:

As the Nativity Set journeys around the community, ask the family who is delivering the set to read Welcome Prayer 1 and invite the next host family to say 'Amen'. When the Nativity Set is handed to the new host family, the new host family then reads Welcome Prayer 2. These prayers can be printed on the back of the Nativity Story sheet.

Christmas Eve:

Create a special place in church to receive the Nativity Set. Invite the host families to the service or event and allow a time for story sharing between the hosts to discover what may have happened whilst the Nativity Set was in their home.

Messy memory

When I invited my own Messy Church to be host households for a Nativity Set, I expected to receive phone calls informing me of difficulties with physically delivering a set or declaring lost Nativity figures. But I heard nothing. Every day I prayed for a safe journey. On Christmas Eve, at our church Christingle Service, the family who had received the Nativity Set on the final day walked down the aisle together, holding the box containing it.

As the congregation sang a Christmas carol this family set up the set on a low table in the middle front of the church chancel. They carefully positioned each piece of the set and quietly sat down in a pew. I was amazed. The journey had been successful. It was now complete. As I turned in my own pew to look around the congregation I could see small knitted sheep being held by young and old. Some had chosen a white sheep, some had chosen black… and someone had chosen the blue one!

Nativity Set suggestions

Now's not the time to fish out of the loft that special cut-glass representation of the Nativity! You need a solid, robust set, perhaps wooden. I used a toy set with lots of PlayMobil® extra bits and pieces. See:

www.playmobil.co.uk

www.fisher-price.com

www.stmichaelsworkshop.co.uk (Godly Play Holy Family)

www.morethangifts.co.uk

Messy Nativity Journey Rota sheet

Day	Date	Name	Address	Phone	Need transport?
	01 Dec				
	02 Dec				
	03 Dec				
	04 Dec				
	05 Dec				
	06 Dec				
	07 Dec				
	08 Dec				
	09 Dec				
	10 Dec				
	11 Dec				
	12 Dec				
	13 Dec				
	14 Dec				
	15 Dec				
	16 Dec				
	17 Dec				
	18 Dec				
	19 Dec				
	20 Dec				
	21 Dec				
	22 Dec				
	23 Dec				
	24 Dec				

Messy Nativity Set prayer sheet

To be read by a member of the household delivering the Nativity Set to the next host household on the Journey Rota:

Welcome Prayer 1

As you welcome this Nativity Set into your home, may you welcome the Lord Jesus into your hearts and lives this Christmas.

The household receiving the Nativity Set say, 'Amen'.

To be read by the new host household:

Welcome Prayer 2

Lord God, we pray for all those travelling this Advent time, to school, to work and visiting. We welcome these figures from the Nativity and pray that you will bless this house and all who live here. Amen.

Messy Nativity Set instruction sheet (for inside the Nativity Set)

Each household needs:

- Nativity Set and box
- Prayer sheet
- Journey Rota sheet
- Nativity Story sheet
- Bag of small knitted sheep

What to do as you receive this set

Find the prayer sheet. The person passing on the set reads the first prayer and you respond 'Amen'. You then read the second prayer. Place back in the box.

Set up the Nativity Set somewhere in your home and read the Nativity Story.

Choose one small knitted sheep, to keep, from the sheep bag.

Keep one of the Nativity Story photocopy sheets.

Take a photograph of the set (optional*).

*Any photos may be used, with your permission, in church publications.

Look on the Journey Rota sheet and contact the next household to arrange delivery of the Messy Nativity Set.

Make sure every piece of the Nativity Set is packed away for the next part of its journey.

Enjoy!

Thank you for taking part in the Messy Nativity Set Journey.

If you have any difficulties please contact .... [name] on .... [telephone number]

Chapter 4: The Messy Street Nativity

The final part of the Messy Nativity Project was a bit scary for me. I knew I couldn't perform the Nativity Story all on my own. Well, actually I once did! When I was a nursery teacher I narrated the whole of the Nativity play while each and every child stood and stared into the audience with stage fright. I've never forgotten it. This time I knew I needed help.

So I approached what was then a new pioneer ministry in Liverpool city centre called River in the City. Pioneer minister Revd Keith Hitchman was very enthusiastic about taking the Nativity story into the street, and we planned a couple of meetings, inviting other interested people along. As word spread about our plans we were invited to a meeting of city centre chaplains. They were delighted to pray for the project and encouraged us greatly. One chaplain and member of Mission in the Economy invited us to join in with her city centre indoor market mission. At the end of a week of mission, could we perform a Nativity in the marketplace, repeating it in different locations just before Christmas Day?

Someone from Liverpool Anglican Cathedral asked if the Sunday School children could join us to sing carols. Liverpool Mothers' Union was invited to be present and help give out tracts and MU family magazines. We chose a short script from www.sgmlifewords.com and packed it out with carols and simple props. The main prop was a lightweight stand-up Nativity scene (with sheep, of course!) that I had been given by Silent Lights (www.silentlights.co.uk) at a Christian Resources Exhibition. A donation to charity sealed the deal, and we focused our attention on Mary, Joseph and Jesus. We aimed to encourage passers-by to volunteer to be Nativity characters.

As word of our messy story continued to spread, we were approached by local radio and newspapers. We performed the Messy Nativity twice in the indoor market, with market stallholders volunteering to be Nativity characters too. Then we were invited to perform once more, outside, on the pedestrian area of the street. Keith braved the cold and narrated the story, in good voice, as we encouraged passers-by to become Nativity characters and engage with the Real meaning of Christmas.

Messy memory

We had heavy snow on the day of the Messy Street Nativity. I was unsure how the project would end, but the determination of the small team won through. Although there were fewer shoppers in town because of the bad weather, we still engaged them with the Nativity story and some followed us through all three performances. God blessed the conclusion of the project and the Messy team who ran it.

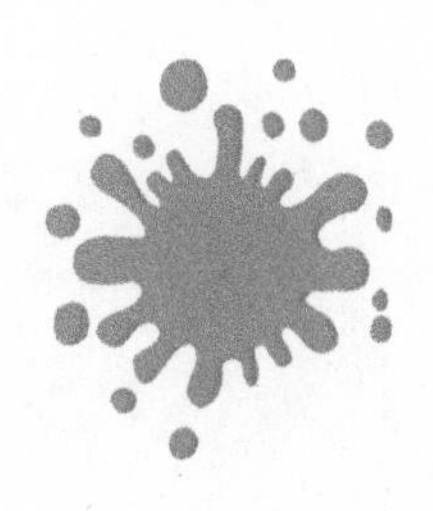

Messy Street Nativity script ideas

Make it short and punchy with a clear message at the end. We used a script from Sgmlifewords, and also ordered some booklets to give out to everyone at the end. See:

Meet the Cast (www.sgmlifewords.com/christmas)

Church Army Posada resources (www.churcharmy.org.uk/posada)

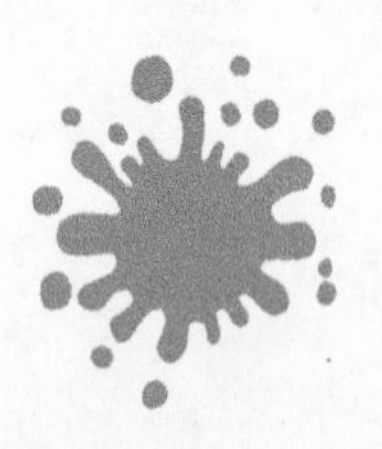

Conclusion

The joy of this messy project is that you can take just one part and enjoy getting the Nativity story heard, whether this is in the home, in shops or on the street.

I'd like to encourage you to try the Messy Nativity Sheep Trail in your town centre, but it could take place anywhere at all—on the high street, in a village, in a market or around a department store.

The Messy Nativity Set Journey could include VIP hosts such as a town hall, cathedral, football or rugby club.

The Messy Street Nativity could be taken to a school, care home or hospital.

There are endless messy opportunities for this project. I hope sharing my story will inspire you to start your own. Please contact Bible Reading Fellowship (BRF), who support Messy Church, if you have any messy stories to share.

Acknowledgments

With thanks to my daughter, Sarah, whose patience and creativity I am in awe of. To my knitting friend, Margaret McDermott, and all the knitters in the many churches and Knit and Natter groups who joined in with this project, especially Bromborough and Eastham Knit and Natter Group, All Saints Church Stand Whitefields Manchester, St Mary's Church Grassendale, Mersey Synod Office staff, Diocese of Liverpool St James' House and Liverpool Mothers' Union. Thanks go also to L19: Messy Church Core Team for being my sounding board and the Church Army for sharing their Posada ideas. Also, thanks to Heather May for her generosity at Silent Lights (www.silentlights.co.uk) and Helen Ellis. Thanks to Liverpool ONE shopping centre management and the twelve shops for allowing me to pilot this project with them.

Thanks to Jonathan Brown, Liverpool ONE Chaplain, and Jean Flood, Chaplain at St John's Market, Liverpool for all your support and encouragement; to Wayne Clarke at BBC Radio Merseyside, who championed the Messy Nativity project so excellently, and to Revd Keith Hitchman at River in the City for his enthusiasm for the Messy Street Nativity. What collaboration! Thank you all for helping to invade Merseyside with knitted sheep and the Real story of Christmas!

Further resources from BRF

Messy Christmas £5.99
ISBN 978 0 85746 091 2

Messy Church 3 £8.99
ISBN 978 0 85746 120 9

Family Fun for Summer £4.99
ISBN 978 0 85746 061 5

Family Fun for Christmas £4.99
ISBN 978 0 85746 063 9

Details are correct at time of going to press and may be subject to change without prior warning.

Starting Your Messy Church

A beginner's guide for churches

Lucy Moore and Jane Leadbetter

Everything you need to know to get your Messy Church going! This resource is for churches who want to see what's involved in starting up a Messy Church, or who are ready to go ahead with one. The book examines:

- Messy Church: the bigger picture
- What Messy Church is and isn't
- Why the shape?
- Why the values?
- Commitment needed to start and run a Messy Church
- Checklist of starting strategies
- Why the network?
- Questions to ask when visiting a Messy Church
- What to expect
- Organising your team
- Sustaining your Messy Church and your team
- Evaluation questions after your pilot period

ISBN 978 0 85746 050 9 £4.99

Messy Church—the DVD

Presented by Lucy Moore

Bringing the Messy Church story to life, the DVD is a resource to help those who are thinking of starting a Messy Church to catch the vision, and, for teams already leading a Messy Church, to help develop good practice and inspire further thinking. It features Messy Churches from a variety of situations across the UK, with parents, children, teens and leaders sharing their experiences and wisdom.

The DVD can be used to:

- Introduce the concept of Messy Church
- Help a new team understand what starting a Messy Church might entail
- Help an existing team think through some of the important issues faced by leadership teams as the Messy work goes on

ISBN 978 1 84101 849 2 £12.99

For further resources to help you make best use of the DVD, visit www.messychurch.org.uk/dvd.

Messy Church

Fresh ideas for building a Christ-centred community

Lucy Moore

Messy Church is bursting with easy-to-do ideas to draw people of all ages together and help them to experience what it means to be part of a Christian community outside of Sunday worship.

At its heart, *Messy Church* aims to create the opportunity for parents, carers and children to enjoy expressing their creativity, sit down together to eat a meal, experience worship and have fun within a church context.

The book sets out the theory and practice of Messy Church and offers 15 themed programme ideas to get you started, each including:

- Bible references and background information
- Suggestions for ten easy-to-do creative art and craft activities
- Easy-to-prepare everyday recipes
- Family-friendly worship outlines

ISBN 978 0 85746 145 2 £8.99

Available from your local Christian bookshop or direct from BRF: visit.brfonline.org.uk.

Messy Church 2

Ideas for discipling a Christ-centred community

Lucy Moore

Messy Church is growing! Since it began in 2004, many churches have picked up the idea of drawing people of all ages together and inviting them to experience fun-filled Christian community outside Sunday worship.

Following the popular Messy Church formula, *Messy Church 2* not only provides a further 15 exciting themed sessions, but also explores ways to help adults and children alike to go further and deeper with God—in other words, to grow as disciples.

As before, the material is overflowing with ideas for creativity, fun, food, fellowship and family-friendly worship, but new to *Messy Church 2* are 'take-away' ideas to help people think about their Messy Church experience between the monthly events.

Across the year, the 15 themes explore:

- Loving God, our neighbours and our world
- The life of Jesus: growing up
- Bible women: Ruth, Hannah and Esther
- Christian basics: who God is
- Baptism: belonging to the family of God
- Holy Communion: sharing and caring together

ISBN 978 0 85746 230 5 £8.99

Messy Crafts

A craft-based journal for Messy Church members

Lucy Moore

This book is a craft book with a difference! As well as bulging with craft ideas to inspire your creativity at Messy Church, it is also a journal to scribble in, doodle on and generally make your own.

The intention is that it will become a scrapbook of conversations, messy moments and prayers—a part of everyday life at home where you can sketch in your own ideas, list useful websites, make notes, reflect on spiritual moments, and journal your Messy Church journey.

ISBN 978 0 85746 068 4 £6.99

Available from your local Christian bookshop or direct from BRF: visit.brfonline.org.uk.

Messy Cooks

A handbook for Messy Church catering teams

Jane Butcher

This book is a handbook for everyone involved in Messy Church catering teams! As well as being a useful treasure store of practical and easy-to-prepare recipes for all your Messy Church events, it also provides tips on quantities, basic cooking skills, essential equipment and ideas for relating food to a Bible story, theme or festival.

There are 36 recipes in total—two delicious main courses and a scrummy dessert for every month of the year. Each recipe includes at least one helpful hint, suggested variations to ring the changes or provide a vegetarian option, and space for you to jot down your own personal reflections, comments and notes.

All the recipes have been used in real Messy Churches, tried and tested in real Messy Church kitchens by real Messy cooks, and enjoyed by real Messy Church families. One Messy cook summed it up by saying, 'We love seeing the children's faces when they come in and ask us, "What's for dinner?"'

ISBN 978 0 85746 069 1 £5.99

Sports Fun for Messy Churches

Lucy Moore

Sports Fun for Messy Churches is a great way to enhance your Messy Church experience by providing fun-filled games and sports activities for families to enjoy together. This book provides a wealth of simple, interactive games and family-friendly sports ideas for Messy Church leaders to use in their sessions. The ideas also pick up a range of healthy living themes.

'Brimming with original, inspirational and fun ideas which will make bodies move, hearts pump and spirits soar. Messy Church and sport is truly a match made in heaven.'
Mark Chester, Founder of Who Let The Dads Out?

ISBN 978 1 84101 824 9 £5.99